NONSENSE
that makes
PEOPLE RICH

Austin Imoru

Nonsense that makes People Rich

First published in 2012
By FineLines Publishers
www.finelinespub.com

ISBN: 9781079438291

for FineLines Publishers

NONSENSE
THAT MAKES
PEOPLE RICH

By

Austin Imoru

Table of Contents

Introduction

It used to be that scarce commodities like precious stones were the only priceless products in our world. Looking at a generation as complex as ours you will realise that things considered as nonsense are twice as priceless. Our streets today are littered with many common, yet priceless nonsense.

In our complex society there are various kinds of nonsense. The most common are the nonsense of the rich and that of everyone else. The nonsense of the rich is largely tied to their expensive mistakes and their laziness.

Your value for what others seems to consider as nonsense will be your greatest advantage in life. These things that are common nonsense to many are precious and priceless. They would pay anything to get rid of their nonsense.

Many are the nonsense that many will be willing to pay for. It is your job to seek out those nonsense and help them find solution to their nonsense. This is what this book is all about, first, to identify nonsense and to help find solution to common nonsense that makes people rich.

Greatest Gift

In our world today, there are so many gifts that so many people will like to over look because it is not what the public terms to be good. The public calls it nonsense but it is a gift that came in the wrapper of nonsense. Yes, it looks like it is nothing but it is something to those who know the value of nonsense.

What is nonsense to you might be a thing of value to another. To some dressing their wardrobe is naturally fun and to other, it is some nonsense they must not waste their time on. What one person would call fun could be nonsense to another.

Therefore, your greatest gift is someone else nonsense, which he or she will be willing to pay for. There things you do naturally; things that are easy for you to do; things that are every day chores for you but to another they are heavy burdens. Consider those things, particularly if they are common nonsense to many people, especially people with means.

Some time ago, an elderly lady told her narrated her story. She was about 73 years of age at the time she told of how her natural happiness was some many rich ladies heavy burden.

It was after she lost her husband in her late forties that she discovered her unique passion for dressing wardrobe neatly. As easy as it sound, it was this nonsense that empowered her financially to build her own apartment in the city of Abuja.

This is not a fairy tale. She found herself financially stranded when her husband died suddenly. She was left with four children with no means of survival at all. At the time she was a full-time house wife, with no education none any special skills. It was then she realise she could work and earn money as house-helps to the wealthy families around her neighbourhood.

Her idea helped a lot and it wasn't long she realised that the three families she was working with love their wardrobes to be kept clean and neat. She also realised that they love to show off their new Jewries and expensive clothes to their wealthy friends. And what normally catches the strangers attention was not the new wears but the cutely arranged wardrobe.

Her greatest gift starts to manifest in a new way. What she loves to do was to keep a clean and neat wardrobe and these wealthy women never could keep their wardrobes neat. Her greatest gift really was the solution to their nonsense. These women were rich women with very lazy nonsense and she was a poor woman with a very unique gift to clean up their nonsense.

Do I need to say she became rich? From the comfort of one client she got recommendations that got her several clients in and out of the city. She would fly from one city to another, all expenses paid, cleaning wardrobes. She built a business out of it – other people's nonsense.

.

Nonsense Attracts Buyers

It was a great eye-opener to realise that very many smart people are making huge financial turnovers from what many would call nonsense. As a matter of fact, many people with money are more willing to pay for nonsense than for any other valuable.

In other words, we have more people going around looking for non-sense to buy than we have those looking for valuables to buy. People with means out there will think twice before giving anyone their money for valuables they are selling. Whereas, the same people wouldn't hesitate to give anyone money for the nonsense they are selling.

Seriously, one good thing about selling nonsense is that you don't even have to know how to sell. As long as you have nonsense you want to sell, buyers will come flocking around. The reason why many of us don't have buyers is because we keep trying to sell what we thinks are good for the people, why running away from nonsense.

All we want to sell are the things that are common in the market. But the problem with common things is that you will have many competitors. However, dealing with non-sense, you will have little or no competitor, because nobody wants to deal on nonsense. Dealing on non-sense will make you the biggest trader; if you like, the one-and-only.

Let's look at it this way, secret buyers are the most expensive buyers. It is known that when your services are highly discreet you attract wealthy and private buyers. Then why is everyone not dealing in discreet services? It is non-sense that service discreet.

I am not suggesting in any way that, discreet or secret are the non-service market out there. As a matter of fact, we need to know what non-sense really is.

It's Nonsense

Ok, let's go to the big question. "What is nonsense?" Non-sense, of course, is not a new coinage we are referring to. It is still the same old coinage in the English Vocabulary. Yeah, non-sense is nonsense. Well, for better understanding, let's look at it as in two broken morphemes; non and sense. Non is an affix for not available while sense is what we can understand or comprehend; another word for attributing meaning to something.

Therefore, when we use the word, nonsense, we are referring to the absence of understanding or meaning, chaotic situations, senseless, absurd, situation void of meaning etc.

Trust me, almost all wealthy people made their money from nonsense. Next time you see nonsense don't ignore it or run away; it might just be that opportunity you have been praying for; your pathway to wealth. As a matter of fact, you have started to believe that what am writing (about) is even nonsense. And if you have not stop reading, it is because you are inquisitive or maybe you are about to stop. Please don't, you are about to make sense of this seemingly piece of nonsense.

Non-sense is something that doesn't make sense. Like most wealthy people who made their wealth through nonsense; all you need to do is make sense out of the nonsense. Those who are struggling to make sense out of the many sense around the world will be more than willing to pay for the sense, you have made out of nonsense. Learn to ponder upon every mess you come across because there is a message in every mess. Your wealth is hidden in the nonsense you can give sense to.

Bill Gate made sense of what to many at the time was a nonsense machine for mathematicians. No software developers could make sense out of the nonsense, so when he made sense out of it, he got heavily paid for the sense.

The likes of Diego Maradona, Austin Okocha, and others made sense of what to many was just a game of leisure and got paid for it. The teacher made sense of nonsense text books; the mechanics made sense of nonsense broken down vehicles; accountants of complex finances and so goes the list of those who make huge fortune from non-sense. They all got paid for the nonsense they gave meaning or sense to.

On every human's complex journey for survival, there is a human nonsense. And whoever can make sense of that personalised nonsense for that human, he or she will be more than willing to pay anything.

Every country, every company, every family, somehow has some kind of nonsense, they require sense for. They will pay anyone that provides the needed sense for their nonsense. Stop trivialising nonsense, make sense of it and get paid. There is nothing like common sense, every little sense is a solution to someone's problem.

4

Your Riches, Their Nonsense

The rich arrive in wealth most of the time with several mistakes and muddy embarrassing situations on their heels. Anyone their can make it go away, make sense out their nonsense will be handsomely rewarded. Are you willing to make their nonsense your riches? First you need to understand how they think.

According to Siebold "**rich people see money as freedom and opportunity** *instead of as the root of all evil.*" If you want to deal with the rich you must realise that they see money as a means to an end not the end in itself. They will spend their health to gain wealth and then try to use the earn wealth to buy a better health. That in itself is nonsense that they are willing to pay for.

The rich understands risk as opportunity to wealth and freedom, you that deal on nonsense should see their risk as your opportunity to provide the cushioning effect when the chips are down. For every risky adventure there is either a cry of pain or a shout of joy. On either case, make sure you are ready to make sense of the nonsense that comes with risk.

You want to be wealthy through others' messes make sure your every move solve a common challenge. Like most rich people let your money and business focus on solution to somebody's mess or nonsense. Make sure that whatever your business is, it solves a problem. At the same time, acknowledge that your goal is to make money from other people's nonsense

Learn to have an action mentality. Once you are alerted of an opportunity, jump at it. Immediately develop an action plan to catch in on it. See opportunity where others see shame and mockery, fear or confusion. Where others see scandal, see discreet and you will attract clients you never thought exist. It will overwhelm you how many people will be willing to pay you to make the excesses of their so-called rich freedom go away.

Seek out what is not common. Learn to look at other people way of life, particularly the rich and constantly ask yourself how you can make it better and easier. Never make the mistake to think that the life of the rich is a perfect one. It is far from it. The bottom-line about them is that they love freedom. Think on how you can give them more freedom, without eating into their time. Thinking this way about the rich will help you outline many nonsense in their lives that you will probably have solutions for.

Working with and for the rich will never let you lack clients for two reasons.

Number one, the nonsense or problems of the rich is common with very many of them. So if you solve (make sense of a nonsense) a problem for one, he will kindly refer his friends to you. Number two, many more are struggling to be rich. They will have the same kind of nonsense, that you already have solution to.

When Henry Ford, made his first sets of cars for the wealthy, he knew that many seemly poor people in his days will struggle to have their own cars. This drove him to carve out a vision to build cheap cars for the many. When I say your riches their nonsense, I mean, unending riches for one nonsense that found sense.

5

Common Non-sense
With Common Sense

I have discovered that if we can look carefully, we will see what others cannot see. The moment of realisation is common to all those who will look a little more carefully. First you must realise that there is nothing like nonsense, only sense that is yet to be discovered.

In this chapter, therefore, attempt has been made to open your eyes to some of those common nonsense that common sense solution is readily available for. You can jump right in and leverage on these opportunities.

1. Pet Care / Training

If you have a pet of your own, this will be the meeting place between your love for pets and the riches you desire. I never thought caring for pets, yield any income until I met an old friend of mine whose business is breeding and selling dogs. He was a true example of a self-made millionaire. Before he explained the business to me, I thought what he successful did in Nigeria was only possible in a country like America where many people love pets, but I was wrong. It can happen anywhere.

Beside breeding pets, you can also choose to care for pets. If you have a pet, it means you already know how to care for a pet, why not turn that skill into profit making and offer to care for those rich folks in your neighbourhood's pets.

More and more people are looking for someone to care for their pets when they can't. Professional pet care givers comes into the home to care for the pet while the owner is away, feeding, walking, and playing with the animal.

You don't need any kind of training or accreditation for this, just your love and maybe knowledge of the pet in question.

2. Residential Cleaning Services

For most wealthy people, cleaning home is one of those things they considered as nonsense. If you can provide that service, they will be willing to pay for the services.

However, home cleaning services is no longer only for the rich. With everyone getting busier all the time, more people than ever are willing to pay to get the benefits of a cleaner home and more free time to do things they consider to be more important.

Residential cleaning services are normally provided on a once-a-month or once-a-week basis. If you're an organized person who can build a clientele, you could do extremely well if you start a cleaning business.

3. Wardrobe Dressing Services

This is a real nonsense business because it looks very ordinary to the less business-minded person. However, if you would take a quick survey of the things that most wealthy women found very difficult to do, wardrobe dressing will probably come up among the first three.

Like most businesses that require good pay, wardrobe dressing comes with very discreet measures. No one will allow you into their privacy if they are not sure you will be very discreet. It is essential part of the wardrobe dressing business.

It can be combined with wardrobe collections recommendation. Since you are experienced in dressing wardrobe for many wealthy people, you will like know what wealthy people wear and why. So you are a likely good resource for making decisive choice when it comes to picking new wears.

Here is cool opportunity to work discreetly with greatness and earn heavily without being spotted. It is an opportunity to be the go-by between wealthy ladies and their stylist, designers and make-up artist.

The pretty thing about working for wealthy people discreetly is that you wouldn't need to go seeking for clients, when they are satisfied with your services, they will recommend your services to their friends and partners. Just make sure you do a good job 'discreetly' and clients will keep coming, from one recommendation to another.

4. Outdoor Cleaning Services

From time to time, those very wealthy one will need someone to help mow their lawns and keep their outdoor clean. You can be that person earning at the expense of the rich.

You might think that all wealthy homes should have their in-house cleaners. Yes, most of them do, but a good lawn mower and pool cleaner is what they all seek. Many people would rather spend the money on having someone else keep their yard looking good. The great thing about this business idea is that in many places, you can combine the two and have a viable business all year long.

You can even include fumigation to your services. It wouldn't be long before they will regard you as a professional. Like the wardrobe dresser, just ensure your work is good and you are very discreet. Yeah, discreet is key in working with wealthy people.

5. Mini-Hauling Services

This is more like running a herald servicing business. There are lots of homes out who need services like this. Call it laziness or whatever you would like to call it, but I call it someone nonsense.

There are loads of women out there, both wealthy and less wealthy who are

tired of going to the market. You can
volunteer to help them do the herald for
them for a token of course.

Build the business around any
herald and light haulage they want done.
Here is a growing business that needs
professional hands right now. You can fill
up the space and make some money.

6. Antique refurbishment

This is a perfect side business for people
who love antiquing. Take worn-out
antiques home with you, invest the time
and care needed to transform those old
items into something amazing, then resell
them at a profit to wealthy people.

You might not know who needs
those things you regards as rubbish or non-

sense. I once met a young man in Lagos, who calls himself, Nigerian Real Estate Champ. He boasted that he can sell anything. This was because he sold an obscure shrine for a whopping $203,000 via eBay.

It was an antiquity that nobody needed anymore. He accidentally sold it while displaying the picture of a piece of land he wanted to sell. Antiquities are precious to some people, find the wealthy people with love for them and you will be in business.

7. Babysitting Services

This is huge business; a real nonsense that many mothers are trying hard to ship out to others who are good at it. If you have free school hours to spear or free evening time, you can do this.

Babysitting may be a great side business for you. Yours could be for only Friday and Saturday nights when young parents would love to hangout without the children. You can earn some solid income doing nothing but caring for someone else child. It could be their nonsense, but your business profits.

8. Bed and Breakfast Services

This has a little risk to it but I'm sure some people can do it effectively well. Now that the price for Hotels and guest house are on the high side, you can use your extra room as a bed for a night hirer.

If there is an old garage in your apartment, kindly cover it into a "bed and breakfast" room for visitors who can't afford to pay for the more expensive guest houses in town. This works particularly well if you have a somewhat older home or live near an area that attracts regular travellers and tourists.

9. Family Dinner Services

There are countless of ladies who claim cooking as their hobbies and they are not making any good use of it. This could be your opportunity to make good use of what you know how to do best.

Several working class women don't really have the time to spend making meal for their homes, you can offer your services to help make their dinner from time to time and charge a little for it.

If you love to cook, this can be a great opportunity, but you may have to put a lot of work into searching for clients.

10. Exercise teacher

It is the era of losing some weight and exercise plays a major role in this. A private exercise instructor will help put most wealthy family on track. I know a lot wealthy families who have lots of family members who have obesity and need some shedding of weight.

If you look physically fit and has a little knowledge of physical fitness or try read up about the subject. Offer to teach a family that are looking really over weight.

Also many gymnasiums will trade membership and often a bit more for a person willing and able to teach an exercise class. If you're in good shape, this is a great opportunity to earn some extra money, plus it can often lead to additional income with one-on-one teaching opportunities.

11. Senior citizen assistance

Many elderly people need assistance with a wide variety of simple household tasks – cleaning, laundry, and so forth. Many children of elderly people are quite willing to hire someone to help out their parents.

12. Teaching music

If you know how to play an instrument (particularly the piano or the guitar) and have patience, you've got what you need to teach others how to play. Offer lessons in that instrument to others – this can also be an excellent thing to barter with, too.

13. Home Tutoring

Did you major in a particular topic in college? Do you have patience with children? You likely have what you need to tutor kids in particular subjects. Seek out parents and let them know that you tutor in a particular subject and provide materials for them to share and phone calls will often trickle in.

6

More Non-Sense

With an estimated N4billion spent daily on the consumption of food, pitching your tent with any or all parts of the food value chain could spin a profit given the right business model and strategy. Whether it is importing, sourcing from the farm gate, hauling, wholesaling, packaging, retailing, catering or exporting, it is pertinent that you possess the acumen to grind out a profit.

Think about starting a restaurant or a raw food stall in your locality.

Some examples of common Nonsense that can make you rich;

1.) Mass marketing of Intellectual products like Audio/Video CDs/DVDs, books, magazines etc. I tell you the truth, this is one huge nonsense that can give you about 50% to 100% profits without any capita or training/skills.

2.) Repackaging business; cooking ingredients like pepper, milk rebranded in gallops, introducing highly hygienic meat shop, selling in scales etc.

3.) Food items shopping: more than a hundred women will gladly sit back home and allow someone do the market errand for them.

4.) School Runs: a huge nonsense that most parents are trying to make sense of. They will be will to pay you handsomely if you save them time, energy and money by helping to get their kids from school.

5.) Cab/Tax Services: today, most would mind what it will take, so long whenever they are ready to go out, they can simply call and you will show up to take them there.

6.) Auto-care Services: many car owners are finding it very difficult to truth mechanics this day. You don't have to be a mechanic, just stand as the trusted middle man. Get the car from the office of the owner to the mechanic, fix it and return it to the owner.

For further information, or to easily contact the author, for anything at all, coaching, questions, speaking engagement or other useful materials, use the addresses below;

P. O. Box 3547,
Benin City, Nigeria,
West Africa.

Tel: +234-708-8925114
         +234-703-8114922

info@austinimoru.com
www.austinimoru.com